THIS WALKER BOOK BELONGS TO:

First published 1983 by
Walker Books Ltd
87 Vauxhall Walk
London SE11 5HJ

New edition published 1988
This edition published 1991

Text © 1988 David Lloyd
Illustrations © 1988 Mary Rees

Printed and bound in Hong Kong by
Dai Nippon (Pte.) Ltd

British Library Cataloguing in Publication Data
Lloyd, David, 1945-
The ball.
I. Title   II. Rees, Mary
823',914 [J]   PZ7
ISBN 0-7445-2017-7

The Ball

WRITTEN BY

David Lloyd

ILLUSTRATED BY

Mary Rees

WALKER BOOKS
LONDON

The ball lay on the ground,
wanting to be thrown.

The ball flew through the air,
wanting to be caught.

A bird caught the ball.
The ball wanted to be dropped.

The ball dropped from the tree.
It wanted to bounce.

Bounce! Bounce! Bounce!
The ball bounced over the wall,
over the hedge, over the cow.
The ball wanted to bounce for ever.

Splash!
The ball bounced into the water.

Bop!
A big fish bumped the ball hard.

The ball rolled towards the girl.
The girl ran towards the ball.

Pow!
The girl kicked the ball.
What a kick!
The greatest kick in the world!

Wheeeeee!
The ball rocketed up
and over the town.

A big black dog came running
out of the town to fetch the ball.

The dog dropped the ball.
The ball lay on the ground,
smiling roundly,
wanting to be thrown again.